The Alphabet Book

Animals

by Steven Brusvale

Note to parents or carers:

Animals are the most diverse group of living organisms on Earth. To date, scientists estimate there are nearly 2 million of animal species. Animals live on land, in water, in soil. Some of them have even learn to live inside other bodies. The animal group includes insects, shellfish, birds, and mammals.

A blue whale, the largest animal on our planet, can weigh up to 150 tonnes and this giant's tongue weights as much as an elephant! Yet many animals are very small in size, and some of them can be detected only through a microscope.

Animals continuously move, eat, reproduce, protect themselves from their enemies, and take care of their offspring. They are part of a food chain, they pollinate plants, distribute fruit and seeds. Animal predators are natural cleaners who control the number of herbivores.

The book contains a careful selection of animal pictures. By looking at them, a child is able to see the general appearance of each animal portrayed with maximum accuracy. This is particularly important in developing the child's understanding of the surrounding world.

I hope this book will make the task of learning an alphabet an exciting and enlightening adventure for your child. Along with your child, you'll be awed, once again, by the variety of animals living among us on this planet.

Steven Brusval

A B C D E F
G H i J K L
M N O P Q
R S T U V
W X Y Z

A

ALLIGATOR

ANT

ALPACA

ANTEATER

ARMADILLO

B

BEAR

BEAVER

BISON

BEE

BUTTERFLY

C

CHEETAH

CAMEL

COYOTE

COW

CATERPILLAR

CAT

D

DEER

DOLPHIN

DONKEY

DOG

DUCK

E

EAGLE

ELEPHANT

F

FOX

FROG

FLAMINGO

G

GIRAFFE

GNU

GOOSE

GORILLA

GOAT

H

HIPPO

HEDGEHOG

HORSE

HYENA

IBIS

IGUANA

J

JACKAL

JAY

JELLYFISH

K

KOALA

KANGAROO

KOMODO
DRAGON

KUDU

L

LION

LEMUR

LADYBIRD

LOBSTER

LYNX

M

MEERKAT

MONKEY

MOUSE

N

NEWT

NUMBAT

OCTOPUS

OKAPI

OWL

OSTRICH

P

PELICAN

PENGUIN

PARROT

POLAR BEAR

PANDA

Q

QUAIL

QUOLL

R

RHINO

RACCOON

RABBIT

S

SHEEP

SQUIRREL

SNAKE

SCORPION

SNAIL

SPIDER

SHARK

T

TIGER

TAPIR

TARSIER

TURKEY

TURTLE

U

URCHIN

UNICORN FISH

V

VULTURE

VAMPIRE BAT

W

WHALE

WOLVERINE

WALRUS

WILD BOAR

WOLF

X

XERUS

Y

YAK

YELLOW-BILLED HORNBILL